Letting Go

Baani Bajwa

BookLeaf Publishing

India | USA | UK

Presentation by *BookLeaf Publishing*

Web: www.bookleafpub.com

E-mail: info@bookleafpub.com

ISBN: 9789358318302

First edition 2024

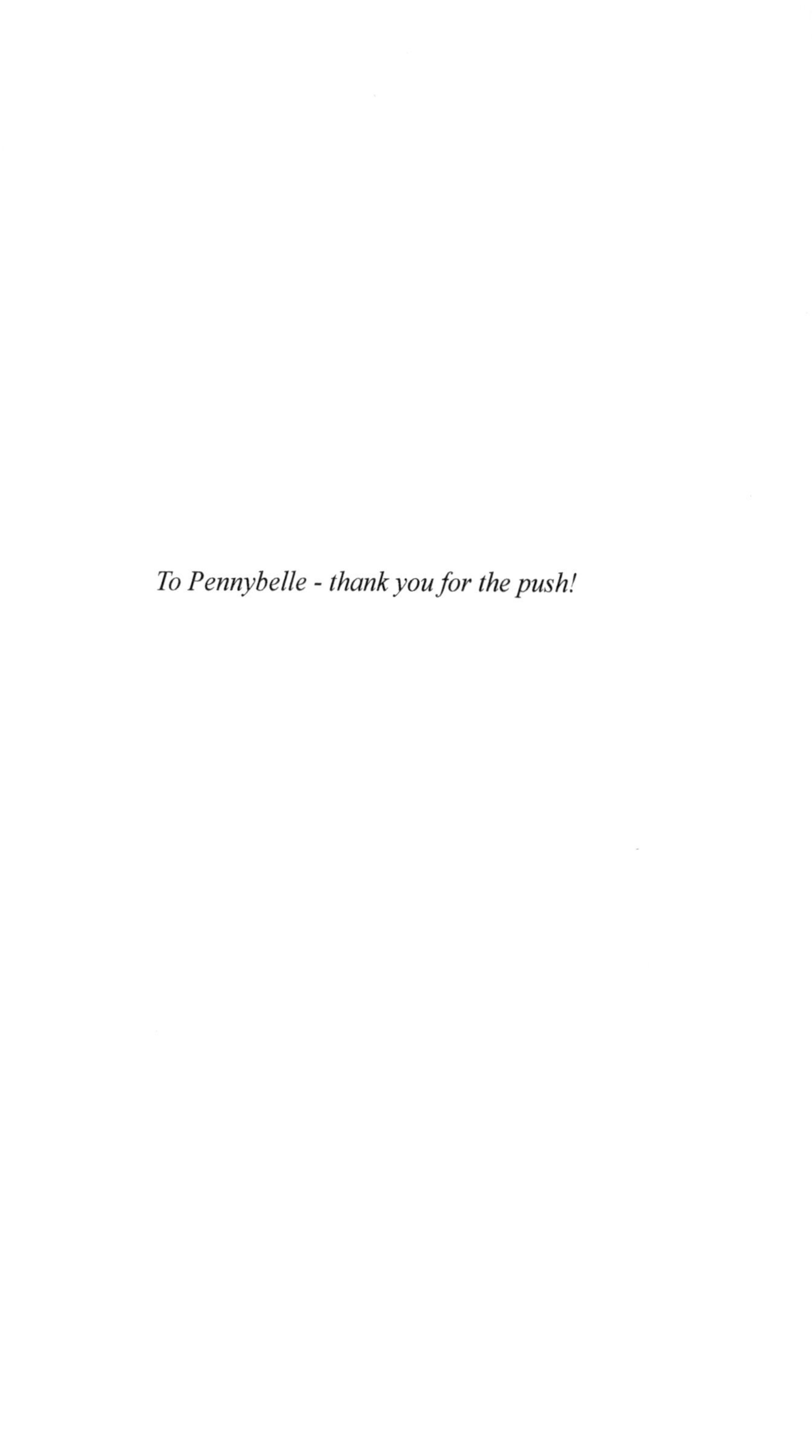

To Pennybelle - thank you for the push!

The People Pleaser

Reject a photo?
I wasn't able,
So we met
across a dining room table.

This was where
the lies began,
I wish I'd known,
I should have ran.

Twelve years on,
the anger remains,
How did I let this happen?
I've suffered so much pain.

"But why?" Might you ask,
"Why not just leave?"
It's not so simple,
You need to believe.

The toxic dynamics,
The gaslighting too,
"So what if I lied?
It was to benefit you!"

"Just trust me" he'd say
But how could I now?
Nothing was true,
He'd conned me somehow.

He'd gaslight and blame,
I fell for it all.
A constant sense of shame,
The start of my fall.

Not Good Enough

Despite having 'chosen' me,
I wasn't good enough,
Ratty hair, weird nails, weird clothes.

Change this, change that,
What will people think of us?
Showing up to places with you!

So short,
So fat,
Too much make up.

Not enough make up,
She's so plain,
She doesn't fit in with us.

I couldn't win,
But what was winning?
Fitting in with these trolls?

Dad

I cried and couldn't leave my bedroom.
I cried for hours alone.
When I finally came down I couldn't hold back
my tears and his dad told me I should go home.

He said it with love, thinking I was homesick.
I was, but that wasn't all. His daughter had been
so cruel, booking me a hair cut without even
asking and belittling to make me feel small.

I'd never cut my hair, but she insisted and
wouldn't take no. She claimed that I was theirs
now so I had to shut up and do what I was told.

I'd never been spoken to so rudely, I couldn't
believe how entitled she was. My husband told
me to ignore her because that's just 'how she
was.'

I went over to my Nani's, my mum met me there
too. I showed them the messages and they both
were shocked. What family had they sent me
into?

I went back later once everyone was asleep, I didn't know how to feel. Did they all feel this way and want to change me, I didn't want to be there anymore.

The next day his dad sat down with me. 'Don't listen to what she has to say, she's jealous of you cause you're perfect. You're beautiful and raised the right way.'

'I haven't cut my hair either, so why doesn't she tell me? From now on I don't want you to talk to her and if she says anything send her to me!'

'You're my daughter now, this is your home, I will look after you, I promised your dad,' so after this I started to feel safe, and had no reason to be feeling so sad.

Until a few weeks later he passed away and our world was turned upside down. This was the start of something, this was when I started to drown.

Inside

It's not always as easy as I make it look
If you knew the strength it took
To just get out of bed

There's a deep sinking sadness
And an overwhelming madness
Battling in my head

Sometimes I feel erratic
And other times ecstatic
I wish that I was dead

The Fly

I sat glaring angrily,
How silly must you be?
Stupid fly, why don't you get it?
I'm trying to set you free!

Why bash into the glass?
The same place! You're not even trying!
That's when I realised,
That's when I started crying.

Trapped but not at all,
This fly is just like me,
Not able to find the strength
To stop, step back, and be free.

Her smile

Her smile lights a room
But the sadness in her soul
Could sink every ship

Where were you?

Where were you when I needed your voice.
I thought we were friends
But I was just a choice.

A choice you didn't make
When I needed you most.

A choice you never made again.

Forgetting

It's hard to forget
Because you made me so happy.

It's hard to forget
Because I thought it was real.

It's hard to forget
Because I felt like living.

It's hard to forget
Because I still haven't healed.

I wonder

I sometimes sit and wonder
If you ever think of me
When you hear a certain song
Or see Mr Bean on TV.

Do you ever sit and laugh
Remembering the silly things we did
Like send that meme every morning
We were just like naughty kids.

Those days really made me happy
You really brought me so much joy,
So thank you for keeping me going
Thank you from me and my boys.

Friend

I help you when you need me,
I call to check up on you,
I travel to keep you company,
I drop everything for you.

But what are you to me?
When I'm crying in my bed,
Crying because I'm hurting,
Crying, wishing I was dead.

You never call to check in on me,
I never have your company,
It is because this mask I wear,
Is placed so perfectly?

I feel so lonely, whose fault is this?
Is it yours or is it mine?
I feel like we'd not even be friends,
If I never called your line.

Mask

It wasn't just them who I left,
It was all of my friends too,
When I'd finally meet them
They'd say I looked happier,
That's when I knew,
I could fool anyone.

Thank you

To those who really loved me
And those who made me laugh
Thank you for keeping me here
Longer than I wanted to.

Don't be sad and wished you could have done
something.
Cause that's exactly what you did.
I would have gone a long time ago
But it was you who kept me longer.

It's not to say you didn't do enough
Cause you did more than your fair share
I just don't have it in me to stay
I never belonged here

So thank you for the good times
I hope you look back and laugh
I love you and I always will
Thank you.

Why?

Nothing comes in straight forward thoughts
Sometimes I'm so happy and singing a tune
Sometimes I'm ready to cry
An overwhelming sadness fills me
Tears ready to spill out of my eyes

Why do I feel everything so fully?
Why can't I be normal like other people?
Why do I remember every last detail of the pain?
Why can't I find the words to release it?

From the outside looking in I look so happy
From the inside looking out I feel so trapped

Who am I doing any of this for?

Sometimes

Sometimes I feel so happy
Only joy in my heart
My babies running and playing
Every moment is just heaven
Their laughter and baby voices
Infuse my soul with joy
My babies, I made them
Every day in awe
So grateful for every second.

Talking to myself

Life goes on
Regardless if you're here or not

But this isn't about you
It's all for them

Your babies need mummy
They love you so much

No one will love them like you
So stay.

You

I'm not always this down
I'm not always this sad
I'm not always this awkward
Not always this mad

I just needed to write
And let out these thoughts

I've been feeling happier lately
I've been wanting to live
I've realised I'm important
And have so much to give

So even when you're losing
You're learning something new.

So sit down and cry
If that's what you need to do
But remember to stand back up
Cause no one else can be you.

Happier

She left everything
Nothing had value in there
Freedom is the price

New start

It's time to say goodbye
To the past and difficult time

It's time to say goodbye
To feeling sad

It's time to say goodbye
To this cold black heart

It's time to say hello
To a new start.